HEAVEN OR HELL: THE LAST JUDGMENT

THE DEVELOPMENT OF CHRISTIAN SYMBOLISM SERIES

An Information Booklet

by

Lois Swan Jones, Ph.D.

Professor of Art History

The Development of Christian Symbolism Series
consists of three fifty-minute, color videos, each supplemented by a guidebook. Authentic plainsong accompanies the wealth of visual material contained in these documentaries .

Volume I: Madonna & Child, 1992, winner of the 1993 CAVE [Catholic Audio Visual Educators] Fine Arts Commendation, discusses the Nativity, the change in the status of the Virgin Mary, the literature that influenced the symbolism, & the artistic & theological changes during the various historical periods.
tape (ISBN: 1-882238-00-1); booklet (ISBN: 1-882238-02-8)

Volume II: Crucifixion & Resurrection, 1994, follows the life of Jesus from the time of his Baptism to his death and Resurrection, emphasizes the Old Testament prophesies that Jesus would fulfill, and discusses and reprints the early medieval play, *Visit to the Sepulchre.* Includes data on the historical and Heavenly Jerusalem.
tape (ISBN: 1-882238-03-6); booklet (ISBN: 1-882238-04-4)

Volume III: Heaven or Hell: The Last Judgment, 1995, recounts Christ's Ascension and return to earth to judge mankind, discusses the influence of the Four Latin Fathers on artistic depictions, & highlights the last book of the New Testament, John's apocalyptic vision of the end of the world. Includes symbolism of the *Majestas Domini*, the winged representations of the Four Gospel writers, Adam & Eve, the Wise & Foolish Virgins, & the Four Platonic Virtues. tape (ISBN: 1-882238-05-2); booklet (ISBN: 1-882238-06-0)

Volume III: Heaven or Hell: The Last Judgment
ISBN: 1-882238-06-0
@ 1994 Swan/Jones Productions

TABLE OF CONTENTS

ACKNOWLEDGMENTS

The Development of Christian Symbolism Series could not have been written without the generous assistance of many individuals. Although I can not name all of them, I would like to single out three people for their continual encouragement, generous gifts of time, and expert advice. Many thanks to

Katherine Lacey Keane

Laura Bowles Allen

Guyanne Tuttle Booth

INTRODUCTION

During the Middle Ages, everything was considered to be a symbol which, if properly interpreted, could make what was invisible to man, visible. As one of the most widely used literary forms for providing insight into symbols, allegory permeated every aspect of theological thinking. Over the years, a four-fold system of interpreting symbols on different levels developed. The symbol had a direct or literal meaning, since it was used to describe or represent something, such as a person or an historical event. Additional meaning was then provided through the use of allegory, tropology, and anagogy. In allegory, the image was viewed as representing something besides what it described, a spiritual or abstract subject. In tropology, the symbol was used to provide a moral lesson; in anagogy, the hidden meaning or ultimate truth of the next world was revealed.

In the story of Abraham and Isaac (which is discussed in the *Crucifixion and Resurrection* video), the Old Testament patriarch's willingness to kill his only son was seen as a prefiguration or an allegory of the Crucifixion, God's sacrifice of his only child, Jesus. Tropologically, the moral lesson was taught that God demanded sacrifices from all Christians. The ultimate truth or anagogical interpretation of the symbol was that in order for Christians to be united with the Lord on the Day of Judgment, they must unquestioningly obey God's laws, just as Abraham had.

Symbols created special significance for every aspect of life, including such things as ecclesiastical buildings, liturgical vessels, colors, and numbers. The church or the House of God signifies the Body of Christ and the Ark in which Noah and his family, as well as other saved Christians, are housed. The foundation of God's temple is faith; the four walls represent the Gospels. The church portal through with the congregation enters symbolizes obedience to God's commandments, an act necessary for salvation. The chalice--the cup used to hold the Eucharist--symbolizes Christian love and faith and represents the Last Supper and Christ's sacrifice on the Cross.

Color is often used symbolically, sometimes acquiring its meaning from Biblical text. **White**--which represents innocence and purity and, therefore, is used by holy or saintly people--derives from a number of sources, including Matthew's description of the angel seated on Jesus's sepulcher after the Resurrection (Matthew 28:3): *his raiment white as snow* and Psalm 50:9 (in the Catholic translation, 51:7 in the Protestant): . . . *thou shalt wash me, and I shall be made whiter than snow.* This is the meaning of the wearing of white by both brides and children receiving their first communion. **Black** is the color of death, the underworld, and the black art of witchcraft. But this opposite of white can also represent humility when used together with the symbol of purity, hence the religious habits of the Dominican monks.

Blue--representing Heaven, Divine love, and truth--became the traditional color for the Virgin Mary. **Red,** so prevalent in blood and fire, is used for martyrs, Bishop's robes, and the Pentecost Season, the time when the Holy Ghost descended to the Apostles. **Purple**, which during the Middle Ages, only emperors and kings were allowed to wear, and thus represented imperial power, was used as a symbol of God the Father. During Advent and Lent, purple can also represent sorrow and penitence. **Green**, an ancient symbol for the rejuvenation of the earth in the spring, is sometime used during Epiphany, the time when the Magi visited the baby Jesus.

Yellow can signify both good and evil. Yellow or **Gold** represents the sun, and divinity, because Jesus said: *I am the light of the world* (John 8:12). But yellow can also be used to show jealousy or treason, as heretics, at this time, were forced to wear this color. Incorporating the former symbolism, *The Development of Christian Symbolism Series* has utilized gold for the background of each video and booklet cover. Blue predominates in *Madonna and Child*; red, *Crucifixion and Resurrection*; and purple, *Heaven or Hell: The Last Judgment.*

Numbers were especially symbolic. The numeral forty, symbol of periods of trials, represented the duration of time when rain drenched the earth during the time of Noah, the Israelites wandered in the wilderness, Jesus fasted in the desert and was tempted by the Devil, and Christ was on earth between his Resurrection and Ascension. Twelve, the sum of the Apostles, can also stand for the Entire Church. Ten represents the Ten Commandments. Eight signifies a rebirth or renewal, just like the musical octave--which derives its name from the Latin word for eight--begins a repetition of the previous seven notes. The most sacred number was seven, a perfect numeral. Not only was this the period of days mentioned in the creation of the world, but it was considered a total number, because seven was formed by adding four--for the Gospels and the directions of the earth--and three--signifying the Trinity and the number of days between Jesus's death and Resurrection. Two symbolized Christ's divine and human nature; one stood for unity.

PROGRAM NOTES

The video, *Heaven or Hell: The Last Judgment* is a fifty-minute program focusing on Christ's Ascension and his return to earth to judge mankind. This program traces the origins and meanings of Christian symbols illustrated by the actual sculpture made during the Middle Ages. The visual material was photographed at numerous sites, including more than forty European churches, most of which are in France, a country where medieval art is still extensive. In order to understand more fully the visual material seen in this documentary, additional information concerning the history, theology, and art of the times is included in this booklet. An explanation of the abbreviations--**B, I, A**, and **M**--is provided below:

B: Biblical quotations in the video and in this booklet are from the Roman Catholic *Douay/Rheims Bible* (1582-1609), the closest to the Latin *Vulgate*, translated by St. Jerome (c. 340-420 AD), which the people of the Middle Ages would have known. The Protestant *King James Version of the Bible* was finished soon after in 1611. Some of the Psalms have different numbers in the Protestant and Catholic translations of the Bible; these are noted.

I: Additional information has been provided for discussion purposes, because the tape could include only the more important aspects of the subject. The script of the tape is not repeated.

A: Art work section provides the location of each work of art shown. All of the churches are in France, unless otherwise indicated. For the small sculptures, the centuries [c.= century] in which they were created and the museums where they are now located are cited. The city of each famous museum is not repeated: The Metropolitan Museum of Art and The Cloisters are in New York City; The British Museum and the Victoria & Albert Museum, in London; the Musée du Louvre and the Musée du Cluny, in Paris. There is a complete list of the sites accompanied by a location map in Appendix A.

M: Musical notations are provided. Heard throughout the video are various masses for the dead, including *Redo quod Redémptor, Omine Iesu Christe,* and *Dies irae (Mass of the Dead)*, which uses dramatic expression and is attributed to Thomas of Celano (died 1250), disciple and biographer of St. Francis of Assisi.

JOHN'S APOCALYPTIC VISION

B: Last book of the New Testament

I: Although a number of apocalyptic writings, which told of the universal destruction of the world, appeared during the first through the fourth centuries, none was as important to Christianity as the vision of St. John, as described in the last book of the New Testament. Usually called the Revelation of John in the Protestant Bible, and the Apocalypse of St. John the Apostle in the Catholic Bible, John sees peace reigning over the end of the world, a time when the battle between good and evil would cease and Christ would return to judge the world. John even mentions the time when the world will end: *when the thousand years are expired.* And as time passed, and the world did not end, the faithful had to consider the exact meaning of John's words.

Writing to seven Christian churches, John describes his enigmatic vision which has had various interpretations throughout history. Seated upon his throne, God has, between his teeth, a sword, symbol for his divine judgment. Bowing down before the Lord, John is provided a key to the past and knowledge of the future. Often illustrated standing to one side, John describes future events, such as the New Jerusalem coming down from Heaven. This Heavenly Jerusalem became a rich and varied symbol, representing life after death. This city which God would provide for the chosen ones was also a symbol for the Christian Church and could be associated with the future role of the historical city of Jerusalem.

John also sees the Lamb of God surrounded by the twenty-four elders, a recurring symbol of the Middle Ages. Throughout John's apocalyptic writings, the book--symbol for authority and power--is emphasized. The mysterious closed book with seven seals is opened by the wounded lamb to show John many wonders: such as the four horsemen of the Apocalypse. During the Middle Ages, the first rider--who wears a crown and carries a bow--was interpreted as a symbol for pestilence; for at this time, it was believed that the plague was spread through the air as if shot by arrows. The second horseman carries a great sword, symbol for war; the third horseman holds a pair of scales and represents famine. The fourth horseman on a pale horse is identified as death. *And power was given him over the four parts of the earth, to kill with sword, with famine, and with death, and with the beasts of the earth.*

John witnessed the great battle between St. Michael and Satan and viewed the site of the final combat between good and evil, Armageddon, and the seductive Whore of Babylon. Because it is described in the Old Testament Book of Joel (3:2), the Valley of Jehoshaphat--usually identified as the Kidron Valley on the eastern side of the city of Jerusalem--was considered the future site of the Last Judgment. The ancient city of Babylon, known for licentious living and moral decay, became a symbol for the political and religious world which was in opposition to the one true Church. It took great vigilance to avoid seduction by the devil, for as Jesus had chastised Peter: *Watch ye, and pray that you enter not into temptation. The spirit indeed is willing, but the flesh is weak. (Mark 14:38)*

Because certain proper names were popular, adjectives were employed to identify important people. Thus in the New Testament, there are John the Baptist, who baptized Jesus; John the Apostle who was at the Last Supper and the Crucifixion; John the Evangelist, who wrote the Gospel According to John; and John of the Book of Revelation, sometimes called St. John the Divine. Although not all scholars today agree on whether or not the last three Johns were one and the same, during the Middle Ages, they were considered one person.

A: 13th-c. Limoges Bishop's Crook, Metropolitan Museum; 12th-c. Nevers, Musée du Louvre; 12th-c. Nevers, Musée du Louvre; Chiesa de San Michele, Lucca, Italy; Montceaux-l'Etoile; St.-Pierre, Chauvigny; two views of a Prince, Münster, Freiburg-im-Breisgau, Germany; St.-Benoît-sur-Loire; Two scenes of Patmos, Greek Island; 14th-c. Crucifixion ivory, Musée du Louvre; *Apocalypse Tapestry*, Angers; 12th-c. *Christ in Majesty*, San Clement, Tahull, now in the Museo de Arte de Cataluña, Barcelona, Spain.

The Apocalypse Tapestry were commissioned by Duke Louis I of Anjou from Nicolas Bataille and designed by Jean Bondon (also spelled Bondol, Bondolf or Jean de Brugge or Hannequin), who was the court painter to French King Charles V. There were seven hangings, sixteen and a half feet wide and up to eighty feet long. Woven in Paris between 1375 and 1379, there were probably originally one hundred five scenes; sixty-seven have survived in part or in whole. During their long history, the tapestries have been used to wrap orange trees and to pad the stalls of horses. These are the oldest medieval tapestries still in existence.

Title Slides: Notre-Dame, Senlis; 12th-c. panel, Musée de Cluny; Cathédrale, Noyon; Carcassonne; Münster, Freiburg-im-Breisgau, Germany; St.-Pierre, Chauvigny; Ste.-Marie, Oloron-Ste-Marie

ADAM AND EVE

B: Genesis 2:7- 3:24

I: The Old Testament relates that in the beginning, sin and death did not exist in the Garden of Eden. *And the Lord God formed man of the slime of the earth: and breathed into his face the breath of life . . . And the Lord God took man, and put him into the paradise of pleasure, to dress it, and to keep it. And he commanded him, saying: Of every tree of paradise thou shalt eat: But of the tree of knowledge of good and evil, thou shalt not eat.* Perceiving that it is *not good for man to be alone*, God took one of Adam's ribs and fashioned the woman called Eve.

The rest of the story is well known, how the first man and women disobeyed God's laws and brought sin, death, and misery into the world. The disobedient pair hid themselves from the face of the Lord God, amidst the trees of paradise. Not only did they disobey God's will, the recalcitrant pair put the blame for their transgression on someone else. Adam blamed Eve; Eve blamed the serpent. God banished all three from the Garden of Eden. God told Eve: . . . *in sorrow shalt thou bring forth children, and thou shalt be under thy husband's power, and he shall have dominion over thee.*

God also rebuked Adam: *with labour and toil shalt thou eat thereof all the days of thy life. . . for dust thou art, and into dust thou shalt return.* The serpent was relegated to be cursed among all the beasts of the earth, and to slither on its belly, eating the dust of the earth all the days of its life. And the serpent's head would be crushed or bruised. This fallen angel can be depicted in many guises: serpent, dragon, demon with horns, deformed winged creature, or a lizard with a woman's face. In the later Middle Ages, Satan was sometimes shown as a prince proffering worldly goods, while only his back side--which contained toads, frogs, and snakes, all symbols of sin-- indicated his true malevolent intentions.

The scene of a man, a woman, a tree, and a snake is a literal interpretation of the Genesis story. In Hebrew the name *Adam* means *man*, a word derived from *Adama* or *earth*. *Eve* translates as *life*, mother of all living things. Adam and Eve became a prefigurative symbol for the redemption of man through the grace of the second Adam--Christ--and the second Eve--the Virgin Mary. Jesus's mother, Mary, is often shown overcoming evil by stamping on a dragon or snake, crushing its head. Although the biblical passage states only that fruit was eaten, tradition later made it an *apple*. Legend relates that the Adam's apple, which is prominent in some men, was supposedly the fruit which stuck in Adam's throat. The story of man's fall from grace also illustrated the three major sins: *lust* in craving the fruit, *avarice* in desiring power and wealth, and *pride* in aspiring to be God-like. Thus Adam and Eve had been tempted, and had succumbed.

A: San Zeno Maggiore, Verona, Italy; Ste.-Eulalie, Elne; San Zeno Maggiore, Verona, Italy; Münster, Freiburg-im-Breisgau, Germany; La Madeleine, Vézelay; San Juan de la Peña, Spain; La Madeleine, Vézelay; 9th-c. ivory, Musée du Louvre; Münster, Basle, Switzerland; Dom, Hildesheim, Germany; San Zeno Maggiore, Verona; Notre Dame, Paris; Cathedral, Salisbury, England; Musée Rolin, Autun; Neuilly-en-Donjon; Notre-Dame, Paris

TEMPTATION OF JESUS

B: Matthew 4:1-11; Mark 1:12-13; Luke 4:1-13

I: After his baptism, Jesus went into the desert where he fasted for forty days and forty nights. During this time, Satan harassed Jesus trying to provoke him into performing miracles to prove that he was the Son of God. Satan first asked Jesus to turn stones into bread. But Jesus retorted: *Not in bread alone doth man live, but in every word that proceedeth from the mouth of God..* Secondly, the Devil dared Jesus to cast himself down from the pinnacle of the Temple. Jesus replied: *Thou shalt not tempt the Lord thy God.* Thirdly, the Devil promised Jesus all the kingdoms of the world, if he would fall down and adore him: *Begone, Satan: for it is written, The Lord thy God shalt thou adore, and him only shalt thou serve. Then the devil left him; and behold the angels came and ministered to him.*

A: two scenes, 12th c.-capital, Metropolitan Museum; St.-Pierre, Beaulieu; St.-Lazare, Autun; St.-Pierre, Chauvigny

THE ASCENSION

B: Acts of the Apostles 1:1-12

I: To the medieval Christian church fathers, it was important to emphasize that Christ was taken bodily into Heaven, and therefore, was, without a doubt, the Son of God.
>
> *And while they were beholding him going up*
> *to heaven, behold two men stood by them in white*
> *garments. Who also said: Ye men of Galilee,*
> *why stand you looking up to heaven?   This*
> *Jesus who is taken up from you into heaven, shall*
> *so come, as you have seen him going into heaven.*

The two men dressed in white are angels. The words--*shall so come--* imply Christ's eventual return to earth.

A: 14th-c. ivory, Musée du Louvre 12th-c. Miégeville Door, St.-Sernin, Toulouse; detail 12th-c. Bury St. Edmund Cross, Cloisters; 12th-c. ivory, Victoria & Albert Museum

M: *Alleluia Mass*, a 12th-century Mass for Ascension Day

THE LORD IN MAJESTY

B: Ezekiel 1:5-10; Book of Revelations 4:1-8

I: Throughout the Middle Ages, one of the most popular representations was the *Majestas Domini* or *Lord in Majesty*. In early artistic depictions, God is seated on two intersecting circles, halos which symbolize Heaven and Earth, his throne and footstool. As Matthew's Gospel relates (5:34-35): *By heaven, for it is the throne of God: Nor by the earth, for it is his footstool.*

This Enthroned Christ represented the Lord's omnipotent power and knowledge and his dominion over the whole world. This forceful symbol--in which the Lord is giving the blessing with his right hand and holding a book with his left--also represented both Christ's Ascension and his return to earth as Judge of the world. Used repeatedly throughout the Middle Ages, the *Majestas Domini* was frequently shown with two angels supporting the Enthroned Lord and combined with symbols for the four gospel writers who had recounted the life of Jesus. Called a Tetramorph (four forms), the gospel writers are usually illustrated with wings and carrying books.

In the fifth century St. Jerome assigned the gospel writers symbols derived from similar visions recorded in the Old Testament Book of Ezekiel and the New Testament Apocalypse of St. John. Matthew is symbolized as a winged man, for his gospel emphasizes Christ's genealogy. Mark is a lion, since his gospel opens with John the Baptist crying in the wilderness. Luke is an ox, because his gospel emphasizes the sacrifice of Jesus. And John is an eagle, to represent the high quality of his gospel's soaring prose.

In his apocalyptic vision (5:8), John saw the Lord on his throne

> *. . . And round about the throne were four and twenty seats; and upon the seats, four and twenty ancients sitting, clothed in white garments, and on their heads were crowns of gold . . .and the four and twenty ancients fell down before the Lamb, having every one of them harps, and golden vials full of odors, which are the prayers of saints.*

The twenty-four Elders represented the authority of the church; specifically the twelve apostles of the New Testament and the twelve heroes of the Old Testament. Harps were illustrated, as were all types of medieval musical instruments. These authorities carried containers full of incense, for the translation of the word *odors* was *incense*. Thus the Lord was surrounded by the church government, composed of Old and New Testament representatives. Depictions of the Elders were often placed upon the archivolts of a tympanum; the number of Elders varies.

A: Panel dated 1020 AD, St.-Genis-des-Fontaines; 12th-c. panel, Museo de Arte de Cataluña, Barcelona, Spain; 12th-c. capital, Marcillac-la-croisille; 12th-c. Royal Portal tympanum with details, Notre-Dame, Chartres; tympanum, Sauveterre-de-Béarn; *Matthew* and *Luke* from Semur-en-Brionaise; *Mark* from Duomo, Verona; *John* from St.-Loup-de-Naud; *Elders* from the following: St.-Pierre, Aulnay; Oloron-Ste.-Marie; Notre-Dame, Chartres; St.-Pierre, Moissac; Oloron-Ste.-Marie

M: *Ubi Caritas (Where is Love)*

THE FOUR LATIN FATHERS

B: Matthew 13:24-42; Genesis 4:3-6

I: In 787 the Second Council of Nicea upheld the use of images for veneration and instruction. These images were to be devised according to the ancient traditions of the Christian Church and the Holy Fathers who had established them. As a consequence, the moralistic programs closely followed the Bible and the writings of the church fathers who had interpreted the Holy Scriptures, especially the patristic authors who lived between the third and the fifth centuries, called the Four Latin Fathers--Ambrose, Jerome, Gregory, and Augustine. To these theologians facts of nature were not important in themselves, but were symbols and principles of ideal truths that provided the foundation for an ethical life. Knowledge was important only in so far as it could help them to know God and could assist them towards salvation for themselves and the faithful. They utilized the allegorical method to interpret the Holy Scriptures.

St. Ambrose (339-397), the Bishop of Milan, wrote a practical guide called *On the Duties of the Clergy* and had his congregation sing hymns, many of which he had composed. **St. Jerome** (c. 341-420), translated the Bible, a Latin version called the *Vulgate,* in the early part of the fifth century. The Hebrew Scriptures, which Christians call the Old Testament, were translated from Hebrew, the New Testament, from Greek. He is also noted for his essays on the perpetual virginity of Mary. Usually depicted with a cardinal's hat, Jerome is either with a lion or beating his breast with a rock while contemplating the crucified Christ.

Pope Gregory (c.540, pope: 590-604), whose name is associated with the Gregorian chants, encouraged monasticism and was concerned with liturgical music. In *Moralia: the Book on Job,* he discussed the virtues and vices. Gregory wrote extensively, but, perhaps, his major achievement was as the transmitter of the doctrines of St. Augustine to the medieval clergy. A prolific writer, **St. Augustine** (354-430), the Bishop of Hippo, wrote *The City of God,* one of the most influential books of the medieval period. St. Augustine did not always originate the theological concepts that he discussed, but he did help popularize them. Since most of the congregation, and even some of the clergy, could not read, St. Augustine's work was transmitted during the Middle Ages, mostly through preachers.

During the Middle Ages, Christian theologians considered that the history of the world was a grand plot conceived by God, a movement from the Creation of the World with Adam and Eve to the End of the World at the Last Judgment. The most momentous historical event was the Incarnation--the coming of Christ to earth in the form of the man Jesus. By the sixth century, this decisive occurrence even divided time--B.C., Before Christ, and A.D., *Anno Domini* (In the year of our Lord). Everything else in history was insignificant. Only the Scriptures, both the Old and the New Testaments, were considered to give meaning to the world; for the most studied book of the Middle Ages was the Bible. While St. Jerome provided scholars with the first adequate Latin translation of the Holy Scriptures, St. Augustine gave direction to their study. Because he often provided both literal and spiritual interpretations for Biblical text, St. Augustine was popular with medieval theologians who believed that all things had a special significance which revealed God's plan for the universe.

In St. Augustine's books everything--history, physical objects, human inventions--are all viewed from the standpoint of how they help Christians understand God's words as expounded in the Bible. This famous theologian considered the Scriptures, when correctly interpreted, to be all the knowledge needed for salvation. Christians did not require any other information. All the answers were to be found in the Bible and in the writings of the church fathers who explained the Holy Book.

A: *Elders,* Oloron-Ste.-Marie; tympanum, Semur-en-Brionaise; Michael Pacher (c. 1435-1498), *Altarpiece of the Church Fathers*, 1462/63, (notice the divine inspiration being provided each Father by the Holy Ghost dove), Alte Pinakothek, Munich, Germany

CAIN AND ABEL

B: Genesis 4:6-12

I: Genesis relates that when it was time to make an offering to God, the younger son Abel, a shepherd, chose the firstling of his flock, the fatted lamb which he offered respectfully with veiled hands. And God was pleased. But God was not pleased with Cain's offering of the fruits of the earth. For the elder son Cain, a farmer, had offered impure wheat full of weeds. *And Cain was exceedingly angry, and his countenance fell.* Full of jealousy and hate, Cain slew his brother and hid him in the bushes. Cain's punishment was:

When thou shalt till [the earth], *it shall not yield
to thee its fruit: a fugitive and a vagabond shalt
thou be upon the earth. Moreover, the Lord set a mark
upon Cain, that whosoever found him should not kill him.*

In his *City of God*, St. Augustine describes two cities: the earthly one
was ruled by the love of self, to the contempt of God. The other, the
New or Heavenly Jerusalem, was built for the glory of God. St.
Augustine interpreted the story of Cain and Abel as a struggle
between the earthly and heavenly cities. Cain, described as evil and
carnal, represented the founder of the corrupt earthly city; the
reverent Abel, the City of God. Moreover, Abel became a symbol
for Christ, the Good Shepherd; Cain, the unbelieving Jew. The death
of Abel, who had offered a sacrificial lamb, can be a prefigurative
symbol for Jesus's Passion as well as a symbol for the Old Testament
Commandment: *Thou Shalt Not Kill.*

A: Expulsion, Cathédrale, Amiens; 6th-c. mosaic (notice the reverse
perspective of the table in order to indicate the bread and chalice on
the altar), San Vitale, Ravenna, Italy; St.-Gilles-du-Gard; St.-Lazare,
Autun; St.-Pierre, Aulnay; St.-Lazare, Autun

WISE AND FOOLISH VIRGINS

B: Matthew 25:1-13

In his Second Epistle to Timothy (4:7-8), Paul wrote: *I have
fought a good fight, I have finished my course, I have kept the faith.
As to the rest, there is laid up for me a crown of justice, which the
Lord the just judge will render to me in that day: and not only to me,
but to them also that love his coming. . .*

I: True Christians needed to be ever vigilant to deflect successfully
the lures of sin and evil. Jesus utilized the parable of the Wise and
Foolish Virgins to illustrate this situation. Matthew tells us that one
night ten virgins waited for the delayed bridegroom in order to enter
the house for the wedding feast. During the course of the evening,
some of the lamps went out, because five of the virgins had been
foolish enough to neglect to bring a sufficient supply of oil. When
these five asked the others if they could borrow some oil, the others
replied that there would not be enough for them all; the shortsighted
ones would need to go to the merchants to buy an additional supply.

While the unprepared women were gone, the bridegroom came. The wise virgins entered the house with the bridegroom, who then shut the door. When the foolish virgins requested entrance, the bridegroom told them: *Amen I say to you, I know you not. Watch ye therefore, because you know not the day nor the hour.* The filled lamps indicated good works; the empty ones, that the owners had neglected their duties. The bridegroom symbolized Christ; the Bride, the Church. The scene indicates that the date of the Last Judgment is unknown. It can be anytime, even now.

A: Münster, Freiburg-im-Breisgau, Germany; église, Corme- Royal; 2 views, Cathédrale, Strasbourg; Notre-Dame, Paris; Münster, Basle, Switzerland; three scenes, Münster, Freiburg-im-Breisgau, Germany

THE SEVEN DEADLY SINS

I: Throughout Christian literature, the analogy is used of Christians as soldiers fighting against evil. In his letter to the Ephesians (6:11), Paul warned: *Put you on the armour of God, that you may be able to stand against the deceits of the devil.* Warriors symbolizing virtues were used to represent this moral battle. In the fourth century, the Spanish poet Aurelius Prudentius Clemens (348-c. 410) wrote an allegorical poem, called *Psychomachia (Battle for Man's Soul)*. The poem describes Christian Faith as leading the virtues, personified as warrior maidens, in a series of seven combats against various vices. This series of combats between the virtues included Faith vs Idolatry, Chastity vs Lust, and Humility vs Pride. For those who had followed the virtuous path, the Crown of Victory was offered. For in his *The Christian Combat*, St. Augustine had written that this crown would be given to those who fight victoriously against the devil. The militant medieval world understood this imagery all too well.

In the Middle Ages, people were especially concerned with God's law and justice as related in the Bible. The Old Testament tells how God gave Moses the Ten Commandments (Exodus 20: 1-17; Deuteronomy 5: 6-21), the divine law for salvation and a code of ethics by which to live. The Ten Commandments, also called the Decalogue, include: (1) *Thou shalt not have strange gods before me;* (2) *Thou shalt not make to thyself a graven thing, nor the likeness of anything that is in heaven;* (3) *Thou shalt not take the name of the Lord thy God in vain;* (4) *Thou* [shalt] *keep holy the Sabbath day;* (5) *Honor thy father and mother;* (6) *Thou shalt not kill;* (7) *Thou shalt not commit adultery;* (8) *Thou shalt not steal;*(9) *Thou shalt not bear false witness against thy neighbour;* (10) *Thou shalt not covet thy neighbour's house, neither shalt thou desire his wife, nor his servant, nor his handmaid, nor his ox, nor his ass, nor anything that is his.* Although the text of these commandments is the same for all Jewish and Christian religions, the enumeration of the list may vary. For instance, in the Roman Catholic and Lutheran churches, the first two are combined while the tenth commandment is divided as to coveting a neighbor's household (Number 9) and coveting the rest of the items (Number 10). Thus, *Thou shalt no kill* is the fifth Commandment in the Roman Catholic religion; the sixth for most Protestants.

All of the Ten Commandments are represented by Moses carrying a tablet. On some Christian churches, Moses is shown with a column surmounted by a winged dragon, in reference to the prophets raising the brazen serpent [Numbers 21:4-9], which became a symbol for Jesus's Crucifixion. [John 3:14-15]. Individual sins were sometimes depicted, such as *thou shalt not kill* which could be represented by Cain killing Abel. A demon pulling out a person's tongue signified one who had blasphemed his Lord. In the Old Testament, death by stoning is prescribed for such sins as idolatry, blasphemy, and Sabbath-breaking. The principle of an *eye for eye, tooth for tooth* (Exodus 21:24; Deuteronomy 19:21) prevails.

The New Testament details some important changes in the way Christians are to live. For Jesus stated that he had not come to replace the Law of Moses, but to fulfill it. [Luke 24:44] When one of the scribes asked Jesus which was the first commandment of all, Jesus answered [Mark 12:29-31; derived from Levicticus 19:18]: . . . *thou shalt love the Lord thy God with thy whole heart, and with thy whole mind, and with thy whole strength.* And then Jesus added a new, more challenging commandment: *And the second is like to it: Thou shalt love thy neighbour as thyself. There is no other commandment greater than these.* Moreover, Jesus emphasized that Christians should *whatsoever you would that men should do to you, do you also to them.* [Matthew 7:12]

Although the New Testament is not explicit as to the punishments sinners should receive in this world, the early church authorities applied austere and strict standards of behavior for those Christians who violated the Church's codes. To assist in guiding these sinners, the clergy required a classified list of offenses accompanied by corresponding methods and periods of penance which should be imposed upon the transgressors. The penitential literature which fulfilled this need was probably developed by the Celtic monks of Wales and Ireland in the late fifth or early sixth centuries. Varying greatly in the penalties extracted, these books were never officially recognized by the ecclesiastical authorities. Some churchmen, such as the members of the Synod of 813 at Charlon-sur-Soane, France, bitterly denounced them. However, because the church authorities had no substitute for these books, they flourished.

As the penitential literature became more prevalent, ecclesiastical authorities needed lists of sins and vices to assist them in formulating the punishments that were pertinent to the transgressions. Although there are some Biblical references from which the list of Cardinal sins derive, the number and order came from the writings of the early churchmen. One of the earliest such compilations was made by John Cassian (lived around 360 to 433), who compiled a list of eight sins and discussed them in his two books--*Institutes of Monastic Life* and *Conferences.*

Writing principally for a monastic audience, Cassian began his list of sins with the three vices--gluttony, lust, and avarice--that were especially dangerous for celibate monks who spent much of their life fasting. Each sin was believed to evolve from the previous one. Thus the severity goes from gluttony to pride, considered the worst of these transgressions. With the Latin term in parentheses, Cassian's list of sins follows:

1. gluttony (*gula*)
2. lust or adultery (*luxuria* or *fonicatio*)
3. avarice or greediness (*avaritia*)
4. anger (*ira*)
5. sadness at serving the Lord (*tristitia*)
6. slothfulness or indifference in religious duties (*acedia*)
7. self-pride or conceit (*vana gloria*)
8. pride (*superbia*), considered the worst of all sins, derived from two biblical passages:

Ecclesiasticus (10:14-15): *The beginning of the pride of man, is to fall off from God. Because his heart is departed from him that made him: for pride is the beginning of all sin: he that holdeth it, shall be filled with maledictions, and it shall ruin him in the end.* (Although Ecclesasticus is in the Catholic Bible, it is only found in the Apocrypha section, if there is one, of the Protestant Bible.)

Proverbs (16:18): *Pride goeth before destruction: and the spirit is lifted up before a fall.*

Cassian's sins gained wide acceptance when St. Benedict (c.480-c.583) founded the first organized European monastery during the sixth century. Benedict compiled a list of seventy-three regulations, called *Regula*, detailing monastic life. One rule provided that each evening a book was to be read aloud. Suggested books included those by John Cassian. This list of sins gained even wider acceptance when in the ninth century, the Synod at Aix promulgated a law requiring all French monasteries to follow *The Rule* by St. Benedict.

Although Cassian's group of basic sins was very popular during the Middle Ages, the list of sins which Pope Gregory the Great discussed in his commentary on the Book of Job, entitled *Morals (Moralia)*, gained in favor, especially among the laity. Gregory changed the order of the vices, dropped slothfulness (*acedia*), added envy (*invidia*), and made pride (*superbia*) the root of the other seven sins. Over the years this list was altered to some extent: the two kinds of pride (*vana gloria* and *superbia*) were combined and the word *tristitia* was replaced by *acedia* (slothfulness). These Seven Cardinal Sins, which gradually began to be used in the penitential literature, were called the Seven Deadly Sins in the latter part of the Middle Ages. These included: pride, anger, envy, avarice, slothfulness, gluttony, and lust. The first five were considered spiritual sins; the last two, carnal.

Monasteries were frequently placed in isolated areas in order that the monks would be removed from the temptations of the secular communities. The monks made vows of poverty, chastity, and obedience in order to combat the sins described in the First Epistle of John (2: 15-16): *Love not the world, nor the things which are in the world. If any man love the world, the charity of the Father is not in him. For all that is in the world is the concupiscence of the flesh, and the concupiscence of the eyes, and the pride of life, which is not of the Father, but is of the world.* The word *concupiscence* is translated as *desire*. The Four Latin Fathers enthusiastically wrote about these temptations, enlarging upon their concepts.

The desire of the flesh, included both *gluttony*, and *lust,* living for sexual pleasures. *Gluttony* referred to excessiveness in any human endeavor, especially food and drink. In St. Benedict's *Regula*, an allotment of about half a pint of wine is suggested, unless the Abbot grants more. Although on certain days the monks fasted, the

Benedictines were allowed sufficient food to enable them to do the manual labor required of those in their order.

Gluttony was also a problem for the laity. During the Middle Ages, there were numerous periods of famine caused by crop failure. The diet of most people was inadequate, lacking in vitamins and proteins, monotonous and dull. Only the rich landowners, who had protected rights to hunting on their forest preserves and to fishing in their private streams, consumed a fairly nutritious diet. The problem of over-indulgence in alcohol was a common form of gluttony. Water was dangerous; wine and beer plentiful. Drowning one's sorrows in a mug of ale was a common devise for coping with life. In art, gluttony could be symbolized by people stuffing themselves with food.

During the Middle Ages, the Latin term *luxuria* meant lust, lechery, or indulging oneself by living only for pleasure. Although the word *lust* implied a strong passionate desire, not just longing for sexual gratification, the symbol for lust was usually a woman with snakes biting at her breasts and often a toad gnawing at her genitals. The snakes are an obvious reference to the one in Paradise; the woman, to Eve. *Lust* and *lechery* with their opposite *chastity* consumed an enormous amount of space in Christian theological literature. St. Augustine wrote at length on the glories of chastity, a basic virtue for priests, monks, and nuns.

The desire of the eyes, or *avarice,* included a craving for money, material objects, and knowledge. Taking an oath of poverty, the Benedictine monks were not allowed to give or receive anything without their Abbot's permission. They followed the example of the Apostles, as reported in the Book of Acts (4:32): *neither did any one say that aught of the things which he possessed, was his own; but all things were common unto them.* Referring to this issue, *avarice* was usually depicted as a man weighted down by money bags, a comparison to Judas, who after betraying Christ for thirty pieces of silver, hung himself.

Paul, who considered *avarice* to be the major sin, wrote in his first letter to Timothy (6:10): *For the desire of money is the root of all evils.* With the development of towns and the revival of commerce in the twelfth century, *avarice* overtook *pride*, as the root of all other sins. *Pride* implied self-love, an arrogance by which all obligations towards God were repudiated. Symbolized by a knight falling from his horse, *Pride* was the pursuit of praise, honor, and power. As with other symbols, this vice also had layers of meaning: it reminded churchgoers of the proud Saul who fell from his horse on the road to Damascus, a sinner who later converted to Christianity and changed his name to Paul.

Prescriptions to overcome these sins were provided for the monks. The remedy for *pride* was prayer, obedience, and humility; for *gluttony,* fasting; for *lust,* celibacy; and for *avarice,* almsgiving. Jesus's parable of the Beggar Lazarus and the Rich Man, called Dives (Luke 16:19-23), emphasizes these sins. Abraham's Bosom, which comes from this Biblical account, symbolized Heaven or the place where the souls of the saints would reside until Christ's death.

Just as vices will be punished, the Bible relates that virtuous Christians will be rewarded. In the Beatitudes recorded in Matthew (5:1-12), Jesus speaks of those who will join the Blessed in Heaven: the poor in spirit, those who mourn, the meek, the righteous, the merciful, the pure in heart, the peacemakers, and the persecuted. In his letter to the Galatians (5:22-23), Paul cites such virtues as charity, joy, peace, patience, kindness, goodness, faithfulness, gentleness, and self-control. Leading a moralistic life brought a Christian closer to God and to Heaven, for St. Augustine (*The Way of Life of the Catholic Church,* Book I, Chapter 15) defined virtue as the perfect love of God.

During the fifth century, a list of Seven Cardinal Virtues was formed by adding the three theological virtues recorded in the New Testament with the four Platonic ones. In his First Letter to the Corinthians (13:13), Paul lists the theological virtues: *And now there remain faith, hope, and charity, these three: but the greatest of these is charity.* The word *charity,* which is translated as *love,* is symbolized by a chalice. Love is the opposite of pride, the sin considered the root of all other transgressions.

The other virtues--fortitude, prudence or wisdom, temperance, and justice--are discussed in *The Republic,* written by the Greek philosopher Plato (427-347 B.C.). These Four Platonic Virtues are also mentioned in the Old Testament Apocrypha Book of Wisdom (8:7 in the Catholic Bible; not in the Protestant Bible, but in the Apocrypha): *And if a man love justice; her labours have great virtues; for she teacheth temperance, and prudence and justice, and fortitude, which are such things as men can have nothing more profitable in life.*

In his *Way of Life of the Catholic Church,* St. Augustine discusses the relationship of God, man, and virtues. *Temperance* is defined as a virtue that allows persons to keep themselves whole and inviolate for God. Practicing temperance, or self-control over one's passion for worldly things, will keep one from the sin of covetousness or avarice. *Fortitude,* or moral strength and courage, allows one to endure all things for God. *Prudence* or wisdom allows one to be able to distinguish the ways which lead to God. Not concerned with the earthly world, but only with the Heavenly sphere, *justice* is considered only in what one will receive at the time of the Last Judgment. For this reason, justice is seen mainly as a means of gladly serving God alone.

A: Two scenes, église, Corme-Royal; St.-Pierre, Aulnay; Carcassonne; *St.-Stephen*, église, St. Just; *St.-Stephen*, St.-Lazare, Autun; Cathédrale, Chartres; Cloisters, Ste.-Eulalile, Elne; *Saint*, Hessisches Landesmuseum, Darmstadt, Germany; St.-Michel-d'Aiguilhe, Le Puy; Abbey, St.-Martin-du-Canigou; cloister, Mont St. Michel; *Saint*, Hessisches Landesmuseum, Darmstadt, Germany; cloister, St.-Michel-de-Cuxa; *Lust*, St.-Jouin-des-marnes; *Avarice*, St.-Pierre, Aulnay; *Avarice*, St.-Lazare, Autun; *Pride*, Ste.-Foy, Conques; *Pride*, Notre-Dame, Paris; *Pride*, Notre-Dame, Chartres; cloister, St.-Pierre, Moissac; *Lazarus & the Rich Man*, 12th-c. side portal St.-Pierre (dated about 1130s), Moissac; *Lazarus & the Rich Man*, capital at La Madeleine, Vézelay

THE LAST JUDGMENT

B: Matthew 24:29-31, 36; Luke 21:25-27; Revelation of John 20:9-15

I: Basic to the Christian philosophy is the coming of the End of the World and the eventual Last Judgment (the spelling, judgement is also correct). The church of Ste. Foy, Conques, has an integrated scene of The Last Judgment. Above the Lord's head are representations of the sun--*Sol*--and the moon--*Luna*. These cosmic symbols represent the universal sovereignty of Christ. The Blessed are always on the favored side, to Christ's right. The dead, who are arising from their caskets to be judged, are depicted nude and at the perfect age of thirty, as described by St. Augustine in his *City of God* (Book 22). Because Christ had lived on earth for three decades, as mentioned by Luke (3:23), St. Augustine believed that the dead would arise at the same age. For this Latin Father wrote that after thirty, man begins to decline towards the defective and duller period of Old Age.

In the New Testament the punishment of sins at the Last Judgment is guaranteed, although few details are provided. The horrors of the fiery Inferno were vividly preached and clearly illustrated in ecclesiastical sculpture. The hideous tortures were made more realistic by the vivid colors that tinted the stone. For this was a time when torture was common and frequently applied. The torments are particularly horrifying. Satan's feet are resting on an indolent sinner, Sloth, who is roasting in the flames; the toad at his feet symbolizes laziness as well as evil. The blasphemer is having his tongue pulled out. During the Middle Ages, it was believed that the condemned would suffer through the organ--in this case, the tongue--that had caused the sin.

A: Ste.-Foy, Conques, dated about 1090 to 1120, received extensive damage during the French Revolution. The villagers decided to demolish the church in 1838, but a Frenchman, Prosper Mérimée opposed the idea and finally saved the church, which today derives much of its revenue from tourist. The Last Judgment Portal contains depictions of 117 people and was repolychromed, probably in the 16th century, when it also may have been moved to its present location.

HISTORICAL CHANGES

Over the time period covered by this documentary, the concept of justice changed radically. It began with concern over justice in the next world, where all would receive adjudication at the Last Judgment.

EARLY MEDIEVAL PERIOD

During the Early Medieval Period, dated about 600 to 1050, the most popular Last Judgment symbol was the *Majestas Domini*, especially those combined with the symbols for the four gospel writers. Carved on small ivories, which could be successfully saved from marauders during those perilous times, these works of art continued in popularity throughout the Middle Ages.

A: Mont St.-Michel; 11th-c. ivory, British Museum; 11th-c. ivory, Metropolitan Museum of Art

HIGH MIDDLE AGES which art historians divide into

ROMANESQUE PERIOD

By the twelfth century, grotesque, often gruesome, depictions of the Horrors of Hell appeared. Usually these scenes were brightly, even garishly painted, making a more distinct and lasting image than the bleached stone does today. In the twelfth century, two great French Last Judgment tympanums were conceived, at the churches of St. Foy in Conques and St. Lazare in Autun. The arising dead who are usually shown nude were difficult to distinguish; consequently, in order to provide incentives for the approved methods of getting into Heaven, the church authorities sometimes added certain attributes to encourage approved conduct. For instance, a cross could indicate one who had made a pilgrimage to Jerusalem or Rome.

A: Two capitals, St.-Pierre, Chauvigny; St.-Lazare, Autun was carved by the master sculptor Gislebertus, sometime around 1125 to 1135. The soft stone is no longer enhanced by polychrome, which once made this Last Judgment more expressive and powerful. Walking under the portal, parishioners could contemplate their future: Heaven or Hell. The sculpture was saved from the destruction of the French Revolution, because it was sealed and hidden from view in 1766 and was not rediscovered until 1837. The head of the towering Christ, who is about nine feet in actual height, was missing. In 1948, when a nearby house was being restored, the head was found and returned to the portal.

GOTHIC PERIOD

During the Gothic Period, roughly dated from about the mid-twelfth century through the thirteenth, the crusades to the Holy Lands continued, but now there were new influences at work: towns were created and expanded, universities and educational facilities were established. There developed, moreover, a growing interest in justice, as it was or was not, meted out by local authorities.

In England, Henry II (1133-1189, ruled 1154-1189), revived Royal justice, sending legal courts into the shires to administer, with twelve local men, the law. This was in sharp contrast to the more traditional forms of justice, such as trial by ordeal or trial by combat. Thus the foundations of the modern English jury system were laid down. Western Europe slowly followed England's legal example. Society became more secular, less concerned with the horrors of the next world, more absorbed with life in the here and now.

The Last Judgment Portal at Notre Dame in Paris provided an artistic shift. In an age when dynasties were becoming entrenched and genealogy was important, clothing needed to be added in order to indicate status. Chain mail for knights and the crusaders; crowns and coronets for the aristocracy. Satan and St. Michael are still weighing the souls, and the devil is still cheating by putting his fingers on the scales. Placed on the archivolts around the tympanum, in a subordinate position, are the depictions of Heaven--Abraham's bosom--and Hell. Once again, a prominent symbol is pride, even though avarice by this time was considered the greatest sin.

Beneath this Parisian Last Judgment Portal are the twelve apostles. For saints were popular as interceders for individuals as well as models for them to emulate. By the Late Middle Ages, each apostle had a distinguishing attribute. St. Peter held his keys to the kingdom. St. John the Evangelist carries his attribute, a chalice by which legend relates he was almost poisoned, but saved by a miracle. Underneath the Apostles on either side of the Last Judgment Portal are small depictions of the virtues and vices pertinent to thirteenth-century parishioners. The small panels above show women carrying medallions on which a specific virtue is represented; below them are the vices shown in essence. Harshness or Baseness versus Nobility or Gentleness is illustrated by a woman kicking her servant. The virtue of Fortitude is the only male figure, a knight in armour holding a shield with a lion, symbol for courage. The opposite is a man dropping his sword and running from a rabbit.

A: Old town of Rouen; University of Cambridge, Cambridge, England; Effigy of Henry II, Eglise, L'Abbaye, Fontevrault; Normandy farm house; Caernarvaon Castle, Wales (Edward II, first Prince of Wales born here in 1284); Altar, Hessisches Landesmuseum, Darmstadt, Germany; Notre Dame, Paris (river view) and details of the 13th-c. Last Judgment Portal

LATE MEDIEVAL PERIOD

The Late Medieval Period is dated the fourteenth and fifteenth centuries in Northern Europe. The fourteenth century was one of the most devastating periods known in Western Europe: about one-third of the population died during the plague called the Black Death, which reached its height between 1348 and 1350. The Italian city of Siena, alone, lost approximately 65,000 out of the 80,000 residents, or about four-fifths of its population. This was also the century of the Babylonian Captivity, when the Roman Catholic Popes lived in Avignon, now part of France, and the Hundred Years War between France and England began.

But by 1453, the 100 Years War between England and France had ended, printing with moveable type had developed, the Moslems had captured Constantinople ending the Eastern Roman Empire, and the translations of Greek authors, such as Aristotle and Plato, changed concepts of the humanities and science. By the fifteenth century, there was a change in attitude toward people's transgressions. By emphasizing the positive, the Seven Virtues, instead of the Seven Deadly Sins, were highlighted. In his *Tomb for Francis II of Brittany and Marguerite de Foix*, Michel Colombe illustrates these gentler ideas.

The full-size corner, female figures represent the Four Platonic Virtues: Fortitude, Temperance, Prudence, and Justice. **Fortitude** means the courage and endurance to choose and pursue the right path. The life-size representation of this virtue wears a helmet and holds a dragon--indicating St. Margaret, who was saved from the dragon who swallowed her when she gave the sign of the cross--and carries a tower, the attribute of St. Barbara, the fourth-century daughter of a pagan nobleman who placed her in a tower so that no man could see her. St. Barbara, who converted to Christianity and added three windows to the tower to indicate the Trinity, was beheaded by her own father for this act of faith. Both of these female saints were known for their courage and fortitude.

Temperance is illustrated by a woman carrying a clock and bridle, indicating a well-regulated life. **Prudence**, meaning wise conduct, is carrying a snake which refers to the saying quoted in Matthew's Gospel (10:16): *. . . Be ye therefore wise* [prudentes] *as serpents. . . .*

The compass indicates her measured judgment; the mirror refers to the wise man who sees himself as he really is. Prudence has two faces like the Roman God, Janus, who looked both backward and forward. Just as people must look where they have been and where they are going.

Justice wears a crown and carries a blunted sword and a book on which are depicted scales. In earlier periods, Christians were occupied with justice in the next world, as provided by the Last Judgment. Now there were those who were concerned with justice in this world as well. The Late Middle Ages had now replaced the horrors of Hell, with the love of the New Testament and thus parishioners moved from a dread of the inevitable towards hope for the future.

A: Siena, Italy, scenes of Palio delle Contrade, a horse race and festival held annually, at which the procession of participants wear 15th-century costumes.

Michel Colombe (c.1430-1515), *Tomb of Francis II of Brittany and Marguerite de Foix,* Cathédrale, Nantes. Colombe was the official sculptor for Anne of Brittany, who commissioned this tomb for her parents. The tomb has effigies of the deceased, with anthropomorphic symbols at their feet. Animals often represented various virtues. The dog here stands for fidelity; the lion, for courage. These animals and their virtues were discussed by the first-century Roman writer Pliny the Elder in his *Natural History* (8:40). Colombe incorporated some of the new Italian Renaissance ideas into this monumental work. The tomb illustrates the Seven Cardinal Virtues consisting of the four Platonic virtues plus the three theological ones--faith, hope, and charity.

UTILIZING THE VIDEO IN A CLASSROOM

It is an educational axiom that people remember little of what they see, and even less of what they hear, but if seeing and hearing are united, more will be learned. This is the impact of television and videos. But it is also an educational adage that for real understanding and for long-term retention, hearing, seeing, and doing must be combined. This is a major reason for using questions and research projects as part of any unified program. The following section provides (1) suggestions for possible ways the video can be divided and shown over several periods of time and (2) some examples of discussions and projects which might be used for different types of audiences.

POSSIBLE DIVISIONS

Heaven or Hell: The Last Judgment can be shown over one, two, or three meetings. Containing a wealth of visual material as well as information on history, art, and theology, this fifty-minute program can be repeated annually. For as they obtain more in-depth knowledge on the subject, viewers will observe different aspects of this documentary. Below are some suggestions for different time allocations.

Three 25/30-Minute Periods

First meeting: show the video from the beginning through the Ascension section (about 17 1/2 minutes).
Second meeting: show the video from the beginning of the *Majestas Domini* section (about 17 1/2 minutes from the start of the program) through the *Lazarus and the Rich Man* section (about 35 minutes).
Third meeting: show the video from the *Lazarus and the Rich Man* section (about 34 1/2 minutes into the tape) to the end.

Two 40/45-Minute Periods

First meeting: show the video from the beginning through the material on The Four Latin Fathers (about 24 minutes). This will leave time for questions.
Second meeting: show the video from the beginning of Cain and Abel (about 24 minutes from the start of the video) to the end, which is about 51 minutes.

SUGGESTIONS FOR STUDY

There are several methods which can be used to encourage viewers of *Heaven or Hell: The Last Judgment* video to take a more active interest. For instance, prior to the showing, assign several people to certain tasks. If possible, include everyone in the room. Such projects might consist of: (1) comparing a more recent contemporary Bible translation with the quotations in the video, which are all from the *Douay/Rheims Bible*, (2) looking for the stylistic changes in the art between the various artistic periods--especially the Romanesque, Gothic, and Late Medieval Styles; and (3) considering the problems faced by medieval artists in illustrating certain theological concepts, such as Heaven, with sculpture.

The group could read the Revelation to John, also called the Apocalypse of St. John the Apostle, and discuss the numerous images used in today's literature and films. Read various translations of this important work.

Discuss the words *law* and *love* and their meanings in the various sections of the Bible compared with present-day concepts of the term. Read the accounts in different encyclopedias,;several are listed in Appendix B.

Discuss the Ten Commandments and compare the virtues and vices popular during the Middle Ages and their use today. Enlarge the discussion to include the differences between mortal and cardinal sins. Bloomfield's book, *The Seven Deadly Sins* (see Appendix B) relates the history of this subject and details the various changes to these sins through out the decades.

The medallions underneath the Apostles at the Last Judgment Portal of Notre-Dame, Paris, illustrate virtues and vices pertinent to medieval parishioners. The virtues derived from St. Thomas Aquinas. Although not shown, the other pairs include Despair vs Hope, Perseverance vs Inconstancy, Prudence vs Folly, Faith vs Idolatry, Charity vs Avarice, Chastity vs Luxuria or Lust, Humility vs Pride, Patience vs Anger, Rebellion vs Obedience, and Discord or Fighting vs Concord or Peace. These virtues and vices can also be discussed in light of the thirteenth century and the present. For more information on this subject see the books by Katzenellenbogen and Male, both cited in Appendix B.

The twenty-four Elders which were placed on Romanesque portals, usually had a similar look. Real distinction was provided by illustrating different crowns, vials, and musical instruments; the last are depictions of particular medieval instruments. But on Gothic churches, these twelve Apostles and twelve Old Testament Heroes were frequently depicted as specific people. In his *The Thirteenth Century,* Emile Male discusses these twenty-four Elders, relating that the churches did not always choose the same Old Testament prophets or kings to be depicted.

The Apostles are listed in three of the gospels--Matthew 10:2-4; Mark 3:16-19, Luke 6:14-16--and the Book of Acts 1:13. Although most of these references provide the same names for the apostles, there is a slight discrepancy. *The Golden Legend* provides the combination of names to produce the twelve: **Simon Peter**; **Andrew**; **Thomas**; **Matthew**; **James**, son of Zebedee, also called James the Greater; **Philip**; **John**, the brother of James; **Bartholomew**; **James**, the son of Alpheus, also called James the Less or James the Just; **Simon** the Cananean also called Simon Zelotes; **Jude and Thadeus** who are one and the same; and the traitor **Judas Iscariot**. On the Gothic Churches, St. Paul replaces Judas.

Study angels; there are a number of excellent books on this fascinating subject, see Appendix B. The Bible has numerous references to angels, many who come to earth to strengthen the faithful in their resolve to do God's work [3 Kings 19:5, Daniel 10:13-21,12:1] and, as Paul wrote in his Letter to the Galatians [3:19], to transmit the law unto them. Angels are particularly important at the time of the Last Judgment, for they protect whatever is consecrated to God. As Matthew [24:31, 25:31] says in his Gospel: *And he shall send his angels with a trumpet, and a great voice: and they shall gather together his elect from the four winds. . . And when the Son of man shall come in his majesty, and all the angels with him, then shall he sit upon the seat of his majesty.*

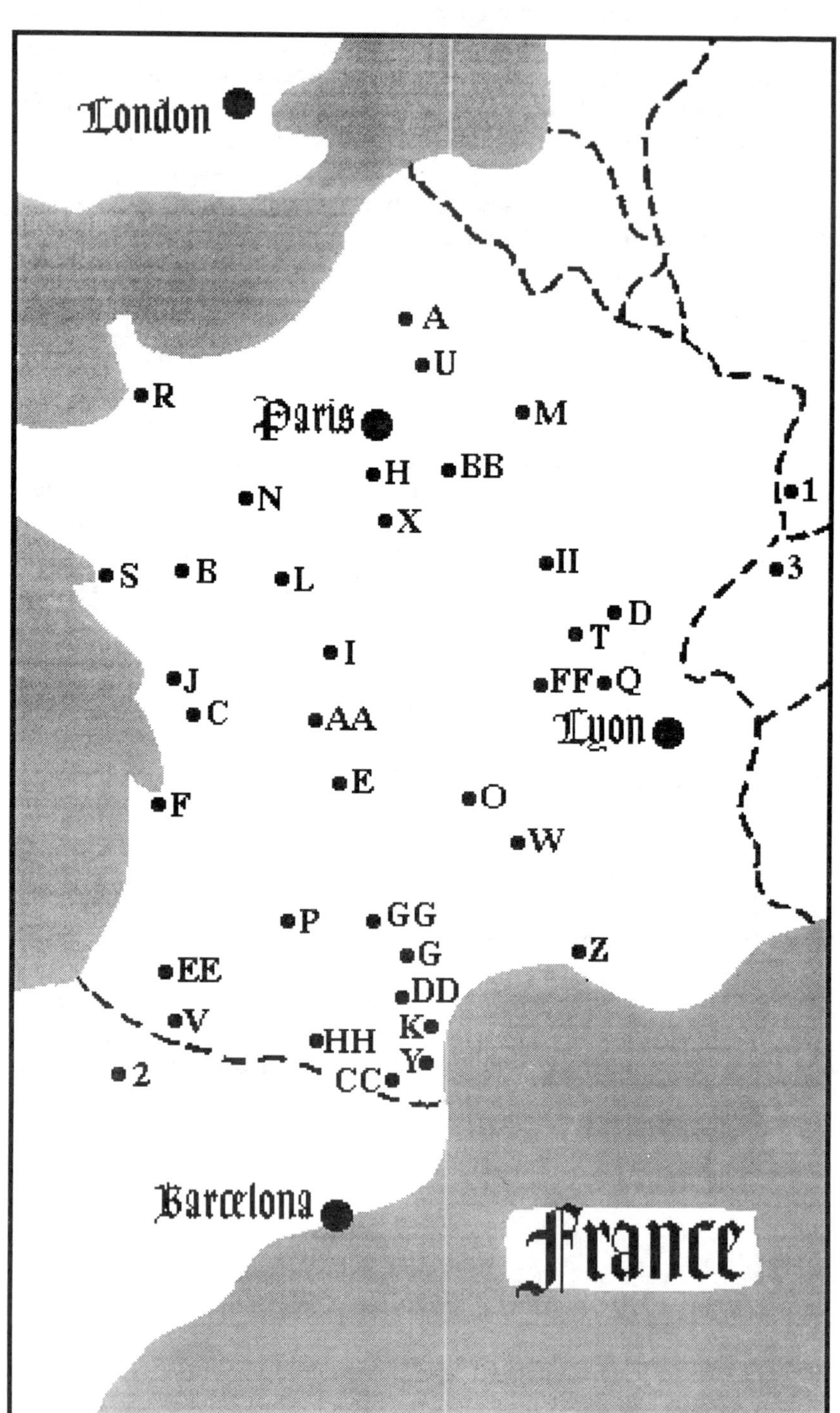

London
Paris
Lyon
Barcelona
France
A
U
R
M
H
BB
N
X
1
II
S
B
L
3
D
T
I
FF
Q
J
C
AA
E
F
O
W
P
GG
Z
G
EE
DD
V
K
HH
Y
2
CC

APPENDIX A: SITES OF WORKS OF ART

Numbers in parentheses correspond to the sites approximate
position on the maps of France and Europe.

ENGLAND AND WALES
Caernarvaon Castle, Wales
Cambridge, University of Cambridge
London, British Museum
London, Courtesy of the Board of Trustees
        of the Victoria & Albert Museum
Salisbury Cathedral

FRANCE
Amiens, Cathédrale (A)
Angers, Château (B)
Aulnay, St.-Pierre (C)
Autun, Musée Rolin
Autun, St.-Lazare (D)
Beaulieu, St.-Pierre (E)
Bordeaux, Cathédrale (F)
Carcassonne (G)
Chartres, Notre-Dame (H)
Chauvigny, St.-Pierre (I)
Corme-Royal, église (J)
Elne, Ste.-Eulalie (K)
Fontevrault, L'Abbaye (L)
Laon, Cathédrale (M)
Le Mans, St.-Julien (N)
Marcillac-la-croisille, église (O)
Moissac, St.-Pierre (P)
Montceaux- l'Etoile (Q)
Mont St.-Michel (R)
Nantes, Cathédrale (S)
Neuilly-en-Donjon (T)
Noyon, Cathédrale (U)
Oloron-Ste-Marie, Ste.-Marie (V)
Paris, Musée de Cluny
Paris, Musée du Louvre
Paris, Notre-Dame

Le Puy, St.-Michel-d'Aiguilhe (W)
St.-Benoît-sur-Loire, Abbaye (X)
St.-Genis-des-Fontaines, église (Y)
St.-Gilles-du-Gard, église (Z)
St.-Jouin-des-marnes, Abbaye (AA)
St.-Loup-de-Naud, église (BB)
St.-Martin-du-Canigou, Abbaye (CC)
St.-Michel-de-Cuxa, Abbaye (DD)
Sauveterre-de-Béarn, église (EE)
Semur-en-Brionaise, église (FF)
Toulouse, St.-Sernin (GG)
Valcabrère, St.-Just (HH)
Vézelay, La Madeleine (II)

GERMANY
Darmstadt, Hessisches Landesmuseum
Freiburg-im-Breisgau, Münster (1)
Hildesheim, Dom
Munich, Alte Pinakothek

ITALY
Lucca, Chiesa de San Michele
Ravenna, San Vitale
Siena, Pinacoteca
Verona, Duomo
Verona, San Zeno Maggiore

SPAIN
Barcelona, Museo de Arte de Cataluña
San Juan de la Peña (2)

SWITZERLAND
Basle, Münster (3)

UNITED STATES
New York City, Metropolitan Museum of Art
New York City, The Cloisters

APPENDIX B: BIBLIOGRAPHY

The bibliography is divided by (1) symbolism resources, (2) historical and Biblical references, and (3) books on angels. For a more complete bibliography on symbolism and a list of hagiographical references, see Jones's book.

SYMBOLISM REFERENCES:

Bloomfield, Morton W. *The Seven Deadly Sins: An Introduction to the History of a Religious Concept, with Special Reference to Medieval Literature.* East Lansing, MI: Michigan State College Press, 1952.

Dunbar, H. Flanders. *Symbolism in Medieval Thought and Its Consummation in the Divine Comedy.* New York: Russell & Russell, 1961.

Ferguson, George. *Signs & Symbols in Christian Art.* New York: Oxford University Press, 1954.

Hall, James. *Dictionary of Subjects & Symbols in Art.* New York: Harper & Row, 1979.

Jones, Lois Swan. *Art Information: Research Methods and Resources.* 3rd edition. Dubuque, IO: Kendall/Hunt, 1990.

Katzenellenbogen, Adolf Edmund Max. *Allegories of the Virtues and Vices in Medieaeval Art.* New York: W.W. Norton , 1964; reprint, Toronto: University of Toronto, 1989.

Male, Emile. *Religious Art in France.* Princeton, NJ: Princeton University Press.
    The Twelfth Century: A Study of the Origins of Medieval Iconography, 1978.
    The Thirteenth Century, 1984.
    The Late Middle Ages, 1986.

Woodruff, Helen. "The Illustrated Manuscripts of Prudentius." *Art Studies* (1929): 33-79.

HISTORY AND BIBLICAL RESOURCES:

Anchor Bible Dictionary. David Noel Freedman, Editor-in-Chief. New York: Doubleday, 1992

Emmerson, Richard K. & Bernard McGinn, eds. *The Apocalypse in the Middle Ages*. Ithaca, NY: Cornell University Press, 1992.

McNeill, John T. and Helena M. Garner, *Medieval Handbooks of Penance*. new York: Columbia University Press, 1990.

The New Catholic Encyclopedia. New York: McGraw-Hill, 1967.

Tierney, Brian and Sidney Painter. *Western Europe in the Middle Ages, 300-1475*. 4th ed. New York: Alfred A. Knopf, 1983.

ANGEL REFERENCES:

Danielou, Jean. *The Angels and Their Mission: According to the Fathers of the Church*. Trans. by David Heimann. Westminister, MD: Christian Classics, Inc., 1976.

Davidson, Gustav. *A Dictionary of Angels, Including the Fallen Angels*. New York: The Free Press, 1967.

Godwin, Malcolm. *Angels: An Endangered Species*. New York: Simon & Schuster, 1990.

Rudwin, Maximilian. *The Devil in Legend and Literature*. Chicago: The Open Court Publishing Company, 1931; reprint: New York: AMS Press, 1970.

Wilson, Peter Lamborn. *Angels*. New York: Pantheon Books, 1980.